I0503889

Quickbooks

Ultimate Guide to Mastering QuickBooks, Step by Step
Bookkeeping & Accounting for Beginners

Table of Contents

Introduction

Quickbooks is one type of business software solution that offers many different types of features for you to use and you can use them as you need it. There are training modules to help you learn features as you require them for your business.

This software lets you manage tasks for your business and manage them easily on the home page. It is very well organized so you can easily find things. Your business is hectic enough as it is, so the software tries to keep it simple.

You can view things essential to your business like your clients, customers, and your financials. Much like mind-mapping, you can make things called workflow arrows to help you connect related tasks visually.

There are different data centers within the software so you can help manage your software. You can access the customer center, vendor center, and employee centers to view and manage essential data quickly and easily.

Also it will keep you on track of your financials. Many business let this fly out of hand pretty quickly. If you're looking for software, chances are you are responsibly or are on the right path. You can use this software to set dates for when things are due and keep track of your budget.

The program also lets you create invoices from included templates so you can have professional looking printouts for your business. It is these little touches that make the image of your business and ultimately affects your customers.

It also lets you seamlessly download your business bank transactions into the software for even better management of your funds and spending.

Quickbooks is a software that is constantly being updated. It's one of the business software solutions you need to keep updated to not fall behind the curve. Recently released from Intuit are new reports.

This allows you to get a quick overview of your expenses and income and much more. The new document management also is a great time saver for letting you keep your documents in order so you can find them in a snap.

CHAPTER 1

Quickbooks For Your Business Need

If you own a start-up business, you've probably heard over and over again that you should get QuickBooks for your business. This can be a great idea for most businesses, but the dizzying array of choices can leave any business owner reeling.

First, consider why QuickBooks should be your first choice.

QuickBooks was the first nationally recognized accounting software program designed for business owners, rather than accountants. Starting in 1992, QuickBooks software has made computerized accounting accessible to every business owner.

QuickBooks uses real accounting methods, but allows users unfamiliar with accounting theory to record business transactions using everyday forms. Most regular business transactions can be entered into the computer by filling out traditional invoices, bills, checks, and deposits.

While the accounting profession in general turned up their nose at this revolution, business owners quickly embraced QuickBooks. QuickBooks listened and learned from its users, and, 15 years later, now has the most widely used accounting software. In fact, I have heard estimates that over 80% of U.S. businesses use registered copies of QuickBooks.

Right now, QuickBooks is really your best option in small business accounting software. Microsoft's Small Business Accounting looks promising, but would not be my recommendation for a start-up business.

If you rarely turn on your computer, don't feel bad or guilty about not buying QuickBooks. If you won't use it, it really is just a waste of money. Find a good accountant who can put your information together on a monthly basis (this is called a write-up service by accountants), and move on to the things you do well.

If you just want to way to save time in certain areas of your business, such as creating checks or keeping track of accounts receivable, you can pair QuickBooks with a write-up service. This is a very good choice for many small or start-up businesses.

If you want access to real-time business information, and are ready to computerize 100%, then find a good QuickBooks accountant to help you set up and maintain your data file.

QuickBooks makes business accounting much easier than traditional accounting packages, but it's best to have a qualified accountant review your file quarterly, at a minimum.

If you want to hire a professional, you can use an outsourcing service to enter all of your accounting details in your file for you, allowing you to use the software as a management tool to monitor company profitability.

The great thing about QuickBooks is that your data file can transfer between types, except online. So, don't worry if you want to use Simple Start. Keep growing your business, and you eventually will be big enough to need the Enterprise version, and hopefully profitable enough to be happy to pay for it!

QuickBooks is not new to any business person specially those who are residing in the marketplace of accounting for a long time. For the enlarging need of precisely handling volumes of data, companies are more focused to offer frameworks where data is maintained boundlessly.

Intuit, keeping the same necessity in mind, has been designed & developed QuickBooks accounting software which is being accessed by businesses to a large extent.

Businesses that are using QB for their bookkeeping related tasks are comparatively more frequent in dealings than those who are not using. There's no harm in accepting some practices which have been forecasted by experts of the industry in order to provide ease of maintaining accounts of your business.

If you are struggling hard to grow your business but unexpectedly fails every time then, there must be any major thing you're leaving behind. In order to fill such gap of mistakes, better you acknowledge certain procedures that will make your QuickBooks accessing more easy & reliable.

Remember, every business catches growth only when it accounts is accurate & holding tight bookkeeping system. After researching many aspects of enriching values in the market, here are six bookkeeping procedures that will help you to understand the power of QuickBooks precisely.

Directly Print Checks: If businesses print checks directly from the software itself then, it saves a lot of time which will later business person needs to invest on preparing reconciliations. It helps businesses to get rid of unnecessary data entry as the software automatically saves the check details and provide right with one single click.

Interlink All Accounts With QuickBooks: The second most needed procedure to maintain your accounts is to reconcile your accounts including, bank accounts, credit cards & other such accounts where you get your statement.

This will make it way easier to track all the transactions made within your business environment. This is the most scalable way to make sure that all the transactions are recorded.

Time-to-time Backup of QuickBooks Data: It is very important for businesses to take backup of all their data in a timely manner as it will save them from data loss like mishappening. QB automates instant backup in a timely manner which doesn't make backups an effort anymore. Users of Cloud-based QB find their data even more secure and backed up.

Gets Access To QuickBooks Online Banking: A reliable way to download all your transactions to QB right from any financial institutions effortlessly.

This allows users to track their transactions and at the same time to save a copy in their own accounting software. Doing this helps them to save time as they no more need to access different platforms in order to get statements.

Set Up 1099 Vendors: Setting up 1099 independent contractors in QuickBooks software makes bookkeeping task much easier as it gathers all the information of your vendors at a single place. This is something that each user of QB needs to keep from the start of their business. Setting up 1099 vendors saves a lot of times in the year-end and helps businesses to mark accuracy.

Integrate Ask My Accountant In QuickBooks: One of the most used platforms by QB users which allows them to rise question-related `to transactions made without any second thought. As this platform reviews all your transaction-related details and helps you to fill accurate taxes.

So these are the top recognized bookkeeping procedures that make QuickBooks unique accounting software than others. In case, you have any doubts related to software accounting or bookkeeping process then, you can connect with experts who are authentic to Intuit's itself.

The basic procedures have been shared but there are still many practices that any business can do in order to enrich their business in the marketplace.

CHAPTER 2

Setting Up Quickbooks

You've just purchased your first Quickbooks software and brought it home. You've been in business for a number of years and figure you can handle entering in your vendors and customers easily. You want to plug it in and start entering your data right away.

The seductive nature of the Easy-Step Interview is calling you and you convince yourself that all you need to do is follow the prompts and you will have a fool-proof QB file in no time.

You aren't quite sure about the Chart of Accounts and you remember filing as an LLC, but aren't sure about whether you should be considered a Sole Proprietorship or Partnership, or S-Corp or C-Corp, etc. STOP!

Quickbooks has been described as a deceptively easy accounting software program. Deceptively, because when you begin entering information and are not 100% sure that you are giving it the right designations, you can really foul up your QB file, and take it from someone who makes a living straightening up other people's QB, it's better to get some help first.

Some information cannot be changed once entered and if you begin using that slightly off item list or chart of accounts, you won't get the desired results on your Quick-

Reports at all and you run the risk of it being un-fixable outside of completely re-entering your file. This chapter and the next few chapters will help you beyond using the Easy-Step Interview and give you the information you need to successfully create your QB file.

I. First Things First

Imagine, if you will, a four square box, or draw it if you like. In the top left box, write in small letters, Sole Proprietorship. In the bottom left box write, again in small letters, Partnership. In the top right box write S-Corp and in the bottom C-Corp.

Each and every one of these types of businesses can be considered an LLC. The LLC is simply a legal designation added to the tax designation of one of the four.

What it means is that if your company is sued, unless you are found to be in gross negligence or doing 'something' illegal, it is very difficult for someone to collect anything. Lawyers typically don't want to mess with an LLC regardless of the tax designation.

It would be bad news for the attorney who does whether he wins or loses the case. If he loses, that is bad enough, but if he wins the judge could appoint him or her as a designated 'partner' of the LLC which means, should your company need to expand you can require payment from your new 'partner' equal to the amount that you or other 'partners' put in, and he/she would have choice but to cough it up.

But if you do really well that year, you can send your new 'partner' a K-1 with income you never paid him/her and he would have to pay taxes on that income you never paid him. So trust me, an attorney doesn't want to mess with you, unless you have done something grossly wrong.

A Sole Proprietorship is one owner, and the year-end taxes are filed with a simple Schedule C and is a much cheaper alternative tax-preparation wise to either of the other three options. Taxes can be filed with your personal 1040 by April 15th.

A Partnership is two or more people running the same business. The Partnership return is filed, like the Sole Proprietorship on April 15th and usually costs more, but not as much as the last two. It, too is filed on April 15th of the tax year.

It is important to get the correct information regarding the percentage shares that each partner has in the business so that at the end of the year each of the income and expense accounts are allocated to the appropriate person. Each is taxed according to the amounts left over after expenses have been paid.

An S-Corp taxes you like a partnership or sole proprietorship, you are taxed once on the amount of income you take after expenses are paid.

In this it is a better arrangement than the C-Corp which causes you to be taxed once on your business' income and yet again on the amount you allocate to yourself when you draw money out to pay your salary. (This can be adjusted or changed for more information contact me at if you need to.)

Having an S or C Corp means your tax return is due on the 15th of March, not April, so you have to be prepared a month earlier than the other. The form that is filed is the 1120 or 1120S and is the costliest of all four options.

II. Which is Best for Your Company?

Which one is right for you depends a great deal on you. If you are working in a field that is ripe for lawsuits, construction, repair, etc, I would suggest the S-Corp or C-Corp to protect your personal assets.

If you are working in the service industry, a Sole Proprietorship or Partnership may work better. If you want that added piece of security against those who see lawsuits as their inherent right to win the lottery, by all means incorporate now!

But if you are just starting out, there is no need to pay well into the $500-600 range to prepare your taxes on what amounts to a hobby until you get more clients.

III. Why Do You Need To Do This First?

1. You Are Going to Need to Assign the Right Accounts

When you determine which designation you are, the QB chart of accounts will assign the right category to the funds you use to start your business and the funds you withdraw to keep it going. Money invested in the Sole Proprietorships or Partnerships is considered an Owner's (or Partner's) Contribution. In a C or S Corp, it is Shareholders Contribution.

When you draw money out from the business that you have put in that is Owner's Draw or Partner's Draw and that money will not be taxed when you take it out because it's a part of your original investment in the company.

Many business owners mistakenly put their initial withdrawals in the salary or payroll expense and end up getting taxed on their own money. In the C or S Corps, money taken out is Shareholder's Distribution and has the same advantage in not getting taxed. The Contribution and Distribution accounts are both part of your Owner's or Shareholder's equity account.

Some accounts when entered and used are difficult to change if entered incorrectly, others must be completely re-worked, so it's important to get these correct!

2. You Are Going to Need to Enter the Right Information

When you enter an account into QB for the first time, you are given the option of entering the tax line. (see part two for explanation for each one.) The first lines on an account are either income or expenses and are broken down as they would be on the appropriate tax for based on which type of return is needed.

Schedule C options are designated as such as are the Schedule E for rental properties, some 1040 lines and K1's. Each of the Schedule C options are for the Sole Proprietorship only. K1 options are for the partnership or corporations and each of the other options make tax preparation very easy for the business owner.

The danger is that these tax lines are optional, QB will work without filling out this information but the Income Tax Report will then only have two categories for transfer to a Corporate or other tax return, Uncategorized Expenses and Uncategorized Income.

And while the numbers won't change so to speak, the taxation of various accounts will and incorrect entries could lead to an incorrect valuation of your business.

3. You Are Going to Need to Start off on the 'Right Foot'

Once you begin using these accounts, it is difficult to reassign transactions to the correct account so you want to make sure that you get started off on the 'right foot'. Like someone remarked once, it's like soup, the more you put into it, the more you get out of it.

Quickbooks is very easy to get started on, but it's important to get the accounts correct as if you don't, you could end up generating reports that are completely useless to both you and the accountant handling your information.

No individual would think it enough to check his bank account once a month, or once a year to verify transactions, he or she would have no idea currently what their financial position is. A business owner should be more cautious and seek to know their financial position on a weekly if not daily basis. It's how you can know what to spend and where.

CHAPTER 3

Entering Accounts To Quickbook

Adding accounts to Quickbooks is very easy, the warning here is that it is so easy that making a mistake either in placement of the account or the identification of where to put it may be a little deceiving.

It is always advisable that you consult a professional to help you as once you add these accounts and begin using them, it can be a long procedure to correct mistakes. And because each business is unique in its accounts, it may take a little creative maneuvering to best fit your type of business. Having said that, let's look at your different options in adding accounts.

I. Income Accounts

There may be several ways that your business receives income. (this is where the help of a ProAdvisor comes in) For example if you are a service industry business, let's use a lawn care company as an example. The overall easy way to handle this is to enter ALL income into one account.

However, this doesn't help you as a business owner decide which of your services is more profitable than another. You may not care about that, but it only takes another few minutes of effort to get it right, so let's make sure we do so. Create an account for income for lawn maintenance, another for landscape design and yet another for pest control or another similar service.

Create a parent account named Lawn Services and a sub account for each of the areas you earn income in. Upon entering these sub-accounts you will see a box labeled sub-account of, check that box and type Lawn Services.

The description, note and tax-line mapping boxes are optional, for the best results however, at least utilize the tax-line mapping and an income account will more than likely fit the first category listed which is Income: Gross Sales or Services. Consult your tax professional for more help with this area.

II. Expense Accounts

The expense window looks identical to the income in every way. I highly recommend a wise use of subaccounts in the expense accounts area as well. For example, grouping your electrical, water and phone bills under utilities is what a lot of businesses do, however, what happens when you add a cell phone?

I would create a parent account for utilities and sub-accounts for power, water, phone, and other utilities. I would also suggest doing the same with advertising expenses, having one parent account for advertising and sub-accounts for signs, yellow pages ads, internet ads, and more so you can keep more careful track of your cash flow.

When you get to payroll expenses, you are definitely going to need to use sub-accounts appropriately and create sub-accounts for FICA payable - Company, Social Security Payable - Company, Worker's Comp, etc. If you do not use Intuit's Payroll services, that's okay, but it increases the risk of mistakes in transmission of information from the payroll companies' to the Quickbooks files.

III. Fixed Assets

There is a step by step procedure in entering fixed assets into Quickbooks and a detailed explanation of how to categorize your fixed assets. Fixed Assets include buildings, land, Machinery, vehicles and Accumulated Depreciation. The only difference in the Fixed Assets window is that the Tax-Line Mapping is automatically entered for you.

IV. Bank Accounts

In Quickbooks a Bank Account isn't always necessarily an actual bank account. When entering a regular bank account whether it's checking or savings, Quickbooks will ask for the opening balance as of a certain date. (If this is a new account, the opening balance isn't necessary, it will be $0.00)

For a more accurate picture of your business' financial situation, and to ensure an accurate reconciliation of your bank account, enter the opening balance, which will be the ending balance of the previous month.

If this account was used for any business transactions prior to the date you install Quickbooks, it would be a good idea to have a Professional help you enter these transactions accurately.

When is a bank account NOT a bank account?

If your business is using petty cash system, (to make change for customers, etc) it is best to set up Petty Cash as a separate bank account so that you can transfer funds from Petty Cash to Undeposited Funds when necessary.

What if you have a customer with whom you have an agreement to trade your services/products with theirs? In this case, you can create a bank account called Trade or Barter and deposit the value of your products/services to offset those of your customers. Neither one are actually bank accounts, but they make it easy to keep track of those 'creative' transactions.

V. Loan

A Loan account keeps track of the amount you owe on loans from those who you owe money to. This is NOT a long term liability account, this is money lent to the business by others and which you intend on paying back within the year.

You have use of the funds, which is an asset, and you owe the loaner, which is a liability. If you need to enter a loan for a vehicle, building, etc, it needs to be in the Long Term Liability accounts.

VI. Credit Card Accounts

You must add a credit card to your account list to gain access to the Enter Credit Card Charges feature on the Quickbooks home menu. Credit Cards can be used to pay for expenses, items or bills. When using Credit Cards to pay bills, one common mistake business owners make is not choosing the correct account to pay the bill out of.

If you are using more than one Credit Card, take it slow and make sure that your payments and credits to the account are appropriately applied or reconciliations will be a nightmare and a half.

You are given the option of being able to enter the account number, expiration date and more as you are entering the card for the first time. As long as you don't have a situation where innumerable people have access to your Quickbooks files, it is perfectly safe to enter this information, if you do have that situation, consider hiring someone else or restricting access to others on your Quickbooks network.

VII. Equity Accounts

An equity account includes owner's draw, owner's contributions, etc (these categories change names but not function, depending on the legal formation of the company). This is the money the business owner invests in order to begin the company and the subsequent money they have to draw from in order to keep the company running.

The retained earnings account is an equity account that is added by Quickbooks at year end when the revenue and expenses are calculated. The description that is given this account by Quickbooks is "undistributed earnings of the company".

In the case of a company just beginning to use Quickbooks, the account can be created manually for previous years balances in another accounting software system by creating the account manually and entering in the opening balance from the previous year.

The rest of the accounts are going to be examined in a separate chapter where we will discuss common mistakes made in entering these accounts and the occasional symbiotic relationship these accounts have with one another.

CHAPTER 4

What To Do With Taxlines

So, I am going to break this chapter into two so that I can be fair to each and every one of you who may be struggling to figure out what to do with that last line in the edit accounts window.

The first part will cover the Schedule C Income and Deductions part of the tax line and the second will examine the K1 and Balance Sheets along with the M-1 and the 8825A-E forms.

I will attempt to make this as informative and entertaining as the subject of taxation will allow. (The IRS doesn't like it when we have fun discussing taxes!)

II. Schedule C Income and Expenses.

Depending on the version of Quickbooks you have, you may or may not see the description 'Schedule C' in the tax line information. Regardless this is the place that you would put income and expenses for your business.

1. Gross Receipts or Sales - You may have as many income accounts as necessary and assign this tax line to them. Whether you call the accounts daily sales, or Credit Card sales, it is revenue brought in to the business by your daily activities.

2. Returns and Allowances - When you purchase items for your business, sometimes it becomes necessary to return them to the vendor. You can't delete the original entry or purchase information but you can record the return using this tax line because technically, though it is not revenue, it is income, because your money is being returned to you.

3. Other Income - This covers income not generated through sales or returns, interest on your business checking account (not investments, that is another line.) charges that you pass on to your clients, bounced checks, late fees, etc. This will help you distinguish what your business is generating on a regular operating basis and will help give you a more accurate picture of your finances.

4. COGS (Cost of Goods Sold) - Purchases - for those businesses that must purchase materials to construct or build products for their customers. A stool manufacturer for example must purchase the legs, the seat, the cushions separately and sometimes from different vendors. A retail store must purchase goods for resale. This is where those purchases must go.

5. COGS - Cost of Labor - These are not salaries, these are the costs of getting the product built and out to the customer. Subcontractors' labor, etc would go here.

6. COGS - Additional Section 263A Costs - This involves the capitalization of certain items of inventory in the possession of the company owner. The good news is that unless the business is producing more than $10,000,000 a year, chances are, this won't apply to you.

7. COGS - Other Costs - If it costs your business to get the item shipped to you or shipped to your customers, that's where this expense goes. Shipping marketing materials, or items for use in your business does not go here.

Deductions

8. Compensation of Officers/Shareholders - If you have your business set up to pay you a regular salary, that amount would go here.

The good news is that most business owners who initially started their companies, if they have put a sizable investment in, can draw out some of their 'pay' in a Distribution to Shareholder category, which means you will only be taking out part of which you put in, and thus, it is not taxable personally to you. A lot of small businesses do not even pay out to the owners until the business is on more solid footing.

9. Compensation of Other Officers - Same as above without the Distribution option unless the 'other' officers are partners who invested in the corporation too.

10. Salaries and Wages - This is of course, where you put in what you paid your employees, not the 1099 vendors, but the weekly, hourly workers.

11. Repairs and Maintenance - This one is self-explanatory, just make sure that your accountant is

depreciating your machinery correctly so that the costs of repairs doesn't escalate beyond the useful life of the asset.

12. Bad Debts - What is a bad debt? When you sell goods or services on account, be aware that some clients won't pay you. Be prepared to either confiscate the goods sold, or continue to bill for services.

At what point does the debt become bad? I'd say probably past 180 days and your chances of collecting are close to zero. There are two ways of handling bad debts in your accounting.

One, the Allowance for Bad Debts account. This assumes that a certain percentage of your Accounts Receivable will turn bad. (.5 - 2%) You create the account in QB and estimate that a certain percentage will never pay and you put it into this account.

Two, only count those who have indicated that they will not pay or cannot pay and add them to the Bad Debts account after 180 days.

Keep in mind that if a bad debt does get paid in a following year, you have to make a reverse entry to take that amount from the bad debt account and put it back into accounts receivable.

13. Rents - Office space, warehouse space, storage space all goes here.

14. State Tax - These are NOT state sales taxes, these are state taxes you pay to operate your business.

15. Local Property Tax - County, City, Parish, etc charges that you pay for to own property in that particular county, city or parish.

16. Payroll Taxes - Quickbooks puts the appropriate payroll taxes here automatically when you subscribe to the Add on service of Assisted Payroll. If you are not subscribed to QB payroll you have to enter in the correct information as to employee and employer contributions to Social Security and Medicare.

17. Other Misc. Taxes - In Northern states that seem to tax residents and businesses out of existence, things like parking taxes, etc would go here. Have you considered moving to Florida?

18. Licenses - Each occupation (legal ones, that is) requires a license to operate. These are usually paid to the county separately from the county taxes. Those fees would be in this tax line.

19. Interest Expense - Are you paying interest expenses? Again, this is self-explanatory.

20. Depletion - This is the natural resources version of Depreciation, so unless your business owns forestry land, oil reserves, or farms, you won't have to deal with Depletion.

21. Advertising - Experts say that unless you are spending 10% of your revenue on advertising, you are not spending enough. However, you have to be wise about it. Any kind of marketing from yellow pages ads (least effective) to radio, television and bench ads would go here.

22. Pension/Profit Sharing - A deal you might make with potential employees is to pay less hourly and pay bonuses based on performance. This keeps a sort of 'ownership'

attitude amongst the employees and the bonuses would be put here.

23. Employee Benefits - Insurance packages, etc would be put here.

24. Meals and Entertainment - When going about your daily business you have to eat. Remember that only 50% of these expenses are deductible, however, if you have a staff party and pay for a meal for all of them, it is all deductible. Oh, and the IRS isn't stupid, you can't have a staff party every day.

25. Other Deductions - If you are unsure of the category and it doesn't seem to fit anywhere above, use this one and be sure to ask your accountant later where it would go.

CHAPTER 5

What To Do With The (Rest Of) The Taxlines

I. K-1 Tax Lines

The K-1 tax form is a little bit like a mutt form on the tax return. Mainly it concerns the division of profits and expenses in a partnership, trust or corporation so if your company is not a partnership or corporation these particular tax lines won't apply to you. Some people receive a K-1 because they are part of a group of people who own a trust or portfolio that generates income through the year.

That income is split up into the designated percentages amongst those in that group. One example of this would be the trust left to a group of siblings that generates income through the year, the eldest receiving 60% and the one or more siblings receiving an equal share of the remaining portion. Each sibling would receive a 1065B which would then be used to fill in the K-1 form.

Schedule K

1. Rentals Income - Used when a partnership or corporation earns income from rental property.

2. Rentals Expenses - Self-explanatory but make sure you can break down what your actual expenses are versus what you think you are spending. Ads, Management fees, mileage to go collect rent or inspect problems with the home, all play a part in reducing your income and tax liability.

3. Portfolio - Interest - CD's - when a CD is part of an investment it earns a special place on the K1 form apart from interest from the US Treasury which is the next category.

4. Portfolio - Interest - U.S. Treasury (bonds) etc. Many of these bonds are non-taxable income and many of these non-taxable bonds pay decent interest rates.

5. Portfolio - Dividends - What would normally be on a 1099 DIV form in the case of a partnership, corporation or trust that owns stock will go on the K1.

6. Portfolio - Royalties - Income received from copyrights, patents, oil, gas or mineral properties. Check

your portfolio to see if your mutual funds are being invested in these type of companies.

7. Other Income - the all-purpose IRS junk category. Other. If you can't fit it into one of the other categories, put it here.

Deductions -

1. Charitable - yes, partnerships, corporations and trusts can donate to worthy causes and receive the same benefits of writing off these donations to offset income and to foster goodwill in their communities.

2. Other - If you can't fit a deduction anywhere else, put it here.

Investment Interest

1. Foreign Tax - Some mutual funds invest globally and thus you end up paying some foreign taxes. Sometimes these foreign taxes are deductible, that is a completely different chapter I haven't written as of yet.

2. Reduction in Available Taxes - another category put on your 1099DIV at the end of the year. Most companies

will not use this category, I have been doing this for 9 years and have yet to service a client that uses this category.

II. Balance Sheet Tax Lines

While a lot of the lines that have been covered can easily go into this income or that expense category, the balance sheet covers the accounts that would be considered assets, liabilities or equity.

1. Cash - this would be your bank accounts, your cash on hand or petty cash accounts. It would include any account that is immediately available as liquid assets.

2. Accounts Receivable - If you accept payment on credit terms, all amounts that you are waiting to be paid would be classified as A/R. There are companies out there now who will pay cash for your receivables, which in cases of extreme cash flow restrictions would be an option. The percentage you get however will be significantly reduced and isn't an option for a lot of smaller business owners.

3. Allowance for Bad Debts - This is the method I discussed earlier about figuring in advance that .5 - 2% of

your A/R will never pay and being able to claim that as such against your A/R.

4. US Government Obligations - Rare to be used, but if you have back taxes or debts owed to the government on a payment plan or regular payments, use this box.

5. Tax Exempt Sec. - If the company owns any bonds or tax exempt securities, these are assets that pay out based on the 'loan' made to the payor.

6. Other Current Assets - These are assets that can be easily and quickly converted to cash within a year's time, CD's, Bonds, etc.

7. Loans to Shareholders - Just as it is feasible for a shareholder in a corporation to loan money to the company, it is also feasible for the shareholder(s) to borrow money from the company.

Keep in mind that this kind of loan is strictly regulated and is one of the reasons that the Enron executives were more closely scrutinized and prosecuted, because the loans were below market value for excessive amounts that could never have been repaid.

8. Mortgage Real Estate Loans - If your business involves the collection of loan amounts for real estate purchases, this would be the account to put those payments into.

9. Other Investments - Are there any other investing activities that your company participates in that generates income either directly or through depreciation or amortization of assets?

10. Buildings - Your building will be included on the balance sheet as being a positive addition to your assets and their value, the loan for the purchase of the buildings however will be on the liability side. There should be a separate fixed asset account showing the original cost of the building.

11. Accumulated Depreciation - the yearly amount deducted from the VALUE (not the COST) of the building, vehicle, etc. Accumulated means all the previous year's accumulated deductions for this asset. This amount if added correctly will appear on the chart of accounts as a negative figure.

12. Land - Land does not depreciate, however the cost of the land is an asset and should be included in the accounting.

13. Accumulated Amortization -

14. Other Assets - Assets that cannot be put into any of these categories. Intangible assets, like goodwill, etc.

Balance Sheet Liabilities

1. Accounts Payable - These are the accounts you owe that are on credit. This is for products, services or merchandise you purchased on credit.

2. Short Term Mortgages Payable - In a time of extreme cash flow need, sometimes a business owner will take out a short term mortgage with collateral. Short term means it should be paid within 12 months.

3. Other Current Liabilities - All liabilities that will be paid off within 12 months.

4. Loans from Shareholders - When the company is strapped for cash and the owners/shareholders are not the money is put here so that when it is taken out it is done

so as a repayment on the loan from the shareholders, with interest, and is not taxable, apart from the interest gained personally to the shareholder.

5. Long Term Mortgages/Notes - Mortgages on property, notes payable to companies or individuals that don't expect payment within a years' time.

6. Other Liabilities - All liabilities not fitting in other categories go here.

7. Capital Stock - The number of shares authorized for issuance by a company's charter, including both common and preferred stock. Generally the value assigned to each share is $1 but that is up to the individual business owner.

8. Paid In Capital - capital received from investors for stock, also called contributed capital.

9. Treasury Stock - stock reacquired by a corporation to be retired or resold to the public. Not to be considered when calculating an earnings per share ratio, dividends or for voting purposes.

Numbers 7,8 and 9 are usually meant for companies with the intent to sell their stock or go public. For these categories I would suggest getting guidance from a CPA before attempting to undergo that process yourself.

M-1

The M-1 is a form used for corporations with income or assets over $250,000. It is a comparison to the beginning years balance sheet to the end of year's balance sheet. The use of Quickbooks makes this preparation easier as the information flows easily from the Quickbooks file to many different types of tax preparation software. (Lacerte, ProSeries, etc)

The cost of these tax preparation software is usually prohibitive for a company that doesn't specialize in tax preparation, so seek out a preparer that uses one of these two systems.

1. Net Income Per Books - the income minus expenses on books flows through to here.

2. Depreciation Per Books - ditto.

3. Expenses on Books not on Return - consult a tax professional before putting any of your accounts into this category!

4. Income on Books not on Return - again, consult a tax professional before using either of these categories.

8825A-E

If your corporation or partnership owns one or more rental real estate properties, the income and expenses are assigned to one of these accounts. The A, B, C etc are for separate rental properties so you can keep track of up to 5 different properties.

1. Gross Rents - how much rental income did you receive for this property.

2. Advertising - how much did it cost you to advertise this property as being for rent?

3. Auto and Travel - how many times did you travel to the property for maintenance, collection of rent, etc.

4. Cleaning and Maintenance - tenants can sometimes make a mess, how much did the carpet cleaning, painting, etc cost you?

5. Commissions - did you hire someone to help you rent the place? Pay them and deduct it here.

6. Insurance - this would be for property and casualty insurance on the property in case you get sued or someone hurts themselves while living on or exploring your property.

7. Legal and Professional Fees - did you have an attorney draw up the rental paperwork?

8. Interest Expense - generally reported on the 1098 of the property.

9. Repairs - outside of regular cleaning, was anything damaged that needed repairs?

10. Taxes - Real estate taxes, county taxes, etc

11. Utilities - Are you paying utilities to keep up appearances while you are trying to rent the property? Are you paying utilities for the tenant?

12. Wages - do you have someone on staff who is your "property manager"? Split up their wages amongst the properties for accurate bookkeeping! (but pay them with one check.)

13. Misc. Expenses - pest control, security, etc would all go here.

CHAPTER 6

The Proper Use Of Sub-Accounts In Quickbooks

It's that little box below the new account you just entered. The box is labeled 'subaccount of' and gives you the opportunity to create a more organized chart of accounts. Hardly anyone ever uses it though. When is a good time to use it? This chapter will address that issue.

On Fixed Assets

The creation of a fixed asset account involves sometimes as many as five different accounts for the same item. Using a vehicle as an example we will look at what subaccounts to create. First, create an account for the vehicle; it is a fixed asset so name the first one Vehicle Value as your main account.

Next create a subaccount under that main one and call it 'Vehicle Cost', the beginning balance of that account will be the amount you paid for the vehicle, not counting any deposit or trade in amounts. Let's say it's a $20,000 vehicle that would be the balance on the 'vehicle cost' subaccount.

Next, create a subaccount under 'vehicle value' and name it 'Accumulated Depreciation - Vehicle' (you may have to abbreviate). The beginning balance on this will be zero in the first year but it is recorded in the negative. So after the first year, there will be a - $5000 in this subaccount.

When you subtract the cost from the accumulated depreciation, the vehicle value is now at $15000. In order to record this negative amount you need an expense account to take it from.

Create a subaccount of Depreciation Expense and call it 'Vehicle' any subsequent fixed assets with depreciation expenses will be subaccounts under the Depreciation Expense category with the total of all of them showing on the main Depreciation Expense category.

Most companies though don't pay cash for a vehicle so they use financing. To do this you need to create a Long Term Liability account for the vehicle in which the opening balance is the amount of the loan used to purchase the vehicle. This amount could differ from the value in that the value doesn't take these deposits or trade ins into account.

Create a subaccount under Long term liability; name it 'vehicle loan'. Create yet another subaccount under Interest expense and name it 'Vehicle Interest'.

When you receive the first bill, the monthly payment amount should be divided between the 'vehicle interest' and the 'vehicle loan' categories. Assigning the total payment to the loan will result in QuickBooks showing a debt that is paid off that hasn't been.

If there is more than one vehicle, it is good to have a separate expense category for each one so you can have an accurate picture of what you are spending on each vehicle. Under the Auto Maintenance account, create the subaccount 'Fuel - vehicle 1' and 'Maintenance - vehicle 1' (As well as vehicle interest 1, vehicle loan 1, etc.)

Other Expense Accounts

There is a general catch all category called 'utilities'. Create subaccounts for 'telephone', 'water', 'power' etc and make 'utilities' the parent category. This will help you break down individual utilities to more carefully manage your spending.

Income Accounts

If your business has a two or three pronged revenue stream, you may want to create separate subaccounts under sales income. For example, a lawn maintenance company may have income from simple lawn maintenance, sprinkler installations, pest control, etc.

A separate subaccount for each will help you with this situation. With only one account for revenue, it makes it difficult to decide if you need to focus on the most profitable aspects of your business.

A word of caution about using subaccounts. If you didn't start out using them and you have several years' worth of income and expenses that are tied to what would be parent accounts, you would need to back track and assign each of those to the new subaccounts.

This is why it is important to get those accounts right from the beginning and have some help installing your QuickBooks software.

CHAPTER 7

Diagnosing Common Errors - Negative Balances In A-P And A-R

Diagnosing problems in a QuickBooks file is easy once you know what you are looking for. It's usually a matter of glancing at the chart of accounts for anything out of the ordinary.

The problem is that most business owners aren't sure what is out of the ordinary and what isn't. I will explain how to diagnose what the problem is and how to correct the problem once known.

Negative Balances in A/P or A/R

Although this may seem kind of basic for those who have been entering data into QB for a while, for those who haven't this may be new information, so hang in there for their sake. Accounts Payable is the account automatically created by QuickBooks when you enter your first bill.

This is the account that all these amounts go into and from which these same amounts are taken when you pay the bill. More often than not, the clients I see for the first time have a negative balance in the A/P and cannot explain why, nor do they know what to do with it.

A negative balance in the A/P would indicate that YOU owe your vendor money, and though there are legitimate reasons why you would give a credit to a vendor, a refund for extra material sent, etc., most of the time it is the result of a simple mistake. That mistake is the entering of a payment to a vendor without entering the bill that the payment should apply to.

This happens when the data entry clerk is not using the Enter Bills/Pay Bills screens and is simply entering the amounts paid into the check register. Since there is no corresponding bill, (according to QuickBooks) the amount of the check is entered as a credit toward the vendor specified.

Likewise, a negative balance in the A/R indicates that there are customers that your company owes money to. And again, there are legitimate reasons you would credit a customer, but often it is a mistake.

The mistake that is made is that a customer payment is recorded without a corresponding invoice being recorded. If the invoice isn't recorded, then according to QuickBooks, this customer doesn't owe you anything, upon receiving the payment and recording it, you now have a customer you owe money to, but not really.

NOW HOW DO I FIX IT?

As with all questions related to accounting, the answer is, "that depends". If these are current mistakes and the bank accounts have not been reconciled as of yet, the method of correction is easy.

For the A/P, look for the Pay Bills and enter in the same check number that you used earlier and pay the bill in that screen. The little 'oh-oh' screen will pop up telling you that this check number is already used, ignore it and use that number anyway.

When you are done with all of these entries, return to the register and look for those identical check numbers, the ones entered correctly will have BILLPMT in the box below the check number, delete the one without that designation and you will have completed the task.

Fixing the A/R is not much different, (assuming that the reconciliations have not been completed!) enter an invoice dating back to the time of the payment received for whatever that customer ordered. The invoice will counter the credit received and will bring the balance out of the negative to zero, unless the customer of course, still owes you for work done.

WHAT IF EVERYTHING IS RECONCILED?

If the negative balances date back into months that have been previously been reconciled and the bank statements and QuickBooks match, deleting these payments by customers and reentering them applying them to invoices will throw off all reconciliations for the rest of the year. You will then have to re-reconcile the bank accounts and that can be tedious.

For A/P corrections aftr reconciliations, DO NOT DELETE THE BILLS! We have to be a little creative with this so here goes. First, create a fake bank account;

call it Adjustment Bank or First Bank of David, whatever you wish. Go to the Pay Bills screen and use the fake bank account to pay the bills you are sure have already been paid.

Once you have completed the entries, make a fake deposit from an account called adjustment into the fake bank account for that same amount of the already paid bills. This effectively zeroes out the bank account, which you can then make inactive.

For A/R corrections after reconciliations, since the amounts have already been received and deposited into the right bank account that has already been reconciled, simply entering in matching invoices to compensate for the received funds will not affect the bank account, and thus will not affect the reconciliations already done.

Just make sure to tie out the payment to the invoice number you create by using the invoice number in the payment memo box. Since the amount won't change you won't have to worry about affecting the reconciled transactions.

Admittedly, this is not the ideal solution, and if you only have a few of these transactions and it won't require an entire year of re-reconciliations, you should do it the long way. However, this way gets you done sooner and lets you get on with the day to day business you love to do. I hope this helps you with your QuickBooks issues.

Excessive Amounts in Undeposited Funds

Often, upon examining the Chart of Accounts of a new client, you will find excessive amounts in their Undeposited Funds account which typically means that their bank balances will not match their statements and reconciliation is made virtually impossible to do accurately.

The Error

There is a three step process in dealing with customer payments. First, the invoice is created with the items, expenses, etc that you are charging your customer for. The invoice amount is then automatically put into the Accounts Receivable account anticipating that a payment will be received.

Second, when the customer does pay, it must be done through using the "Receive Payments" icon. Once the customer's name is entered, you will see the list of invoices that this customer still owes you money on.

You enter the amount of the payment made and check off the invoice that the customer sent the payment in for. Click on save and close and you have now officially received the payment from the customer for that invoice.

But wait, the invoice now is considered paid according to QuickBooks, so the customer's balance will be what it should be. The amount however, stays in the Undeposited Funds account, which is where QB puts it after the second step.

I have seen as much as four or five years' worth of received payments that have been put into the Undeposited Funds account, and yet have never been Deposited into the appropriate bank account. This third step is what many people miss.

Third, you must click on the Make Deposits icon, group all the payments, checks, etc as you would do on your bank's deposit slips and put them into the account on the day you physically took those checks to the bank and deposited them.

For example, if you receive ten checks and you take all ten to the bank, your bank will record the total deposit, not the individual checks and amounts. When you reconcile the bank statements, the deposits in QB should match the deposits on the statements. So if your bank statement shows a deposit of $10100, the QuickBooks deposit should have a deposit of $10100.

If you have the Intuit Merchant services all the credit card transactions that have been processed will group together according to the day you processed them.

You must click on the 'Get Funding Status' button which will link you to the Intuit Merchant Services site to verify that those payments have indeed been deposited.

If you fail to do this in a timely manner, the information about their funding status is deleted from the Merchant Services server three months from the day you entered them and you will not be able to verify that the amounts have been funded.

A Costly Mistake

What some people have done is that they have 'forced' a deposit into the bank register when their statements don't match, and they still have the excessive amounts received in their Undeposited Funds Account. Now they reconcile the bank statements, and true, they will now tie out nicely, the financial statements will be completely wrong. How?

First, if you are having your taxes prepared using the QB reports, you have now told the preparer, AND the IRS that you have been paid twice as much as you actually have. And you will pay taxes on the money that you are forcing into your bank register as a deposit, and on the money that the customers actually paid you.

Second, now you have to have someone go in to correct these mistakes in the QuickBooks file by deleting the deposits forced in and applying payments received in Undeposited Funds to those deposits. This can take hours depending on how far back the issue goes and how many months need to be corrected.

Third, now you have to reconcile the accounts, because by deleting these forced deposits that you have reconciled, you have thrown the reconciliations off by the amounts you have deleted.

You will have to go into the bank reconciliation screen and click on the 'Undo Last Reconciliation' button until you get to the point at which these errors began to be made. Having a professional do this for you can be upwards of $100/hour and if you calculate at about 2 hours for each month's work that can add up quickly.

Can I Do It Myself?

There is no fast way to do this, but this is the procedure I would follow if I were completing this project. One, print out the deposit detail record going back to the time these mistakes were made complete with the dates of each deposit, the amounts, etc.

Two, use this printout and the 'Make Deposits' button to match the amounts of each deposit for each day it was deposited. Continue until you get up to the current period where you should start receiving and depositing payments correctly.

Three, delete all the 'forced' deposits from the bank register. Be cautious so as to not accidentally erase the corrected deposits. Fourth, using the 'Reconcile Bank' screen click on the 'Undo Last Reconciliation' button until you get to the month where the mistakes began to be made.

If there are several months or years involved here, you still have to go back to the beginning so be patient. Fifth, re-reconcile each month to its own bank statement. This is the right way to do it and you should do it this way if you at all can.

I do not recommend doing it this way! It is much easier, faster and tempting, but doing so can lead to an IRS auditor looking closer into your books than you wish them to and staying longer than you'd like. But yes, there IS a faster way. I have to caution that I do not recommend this in any way, shape or form but here is the easy way.

Choose the month at which you want to begin doing things 'right'. Let's say, October of 2019. Now, create a fake bank account called adjustment bank, whatever you'd like to call it. Go to the Make Deposits screen and click all the received funds from September 20119 to the beginning of the problem.

Make one lump sum deposit for the year into that fake bank account for all those payments that have been received. If it's more than one year's worth make sure to deposit them according to whatever year the money was received.

Make a general journal entry with the fake bank account and debit the fake bank account for that amount of money, the credit would be in the adjustment income account and would delete that amount. Now make that fake bank account inactive and make the adjustment income account inactive after zeroing it out.

Again, I do not recommend this at all, but you are done in less than half the time it would take you to do it the right way. And remember that whichever way you decide to solve this issue, to start and to keep doing it right from now on.

CHAPTER 8

How To Back-Up A Quickbooks Company File

If you use QuickBooks to store and manipulate your company's financial data, it will become crucial that you take steps to protect this data.

Given enough time, the most reliable PC will have some sort of hardware malfunction. You should back up your QuickBooks data on a regular basis to protect against such failure. You have an option to do this manually or to schedule an automatic back-up.

1. Back up your data manually

To manually create a backup of your QuickBooks data follow the steps below:

On the File menu, click Save copy or Back up

If this is the first time you've backed up your QuickBooks data, you may see the Portable Company File Feature dialog box. -Select Do not display this message in the future, and click OK to proceed.

Several storage options exists to store your QuickBooks back up files.

CD-ROMs/DVD-ROMs: CD-ROMs have been around for years and continue to be a viable storage medium for backups. Their affordable price can allow you to make multiple copies of your backup files to store in multiple locations for added security.

Flash drives: Also known as keychain drives or thumb drives; this media can store an incredible amount of data (many versions of backup files) in a small form factor. You could buy a flash drive specifically for backing up QuickBooks files and keep it safe in-between backups.

Offsite Backups: Some internet services (including one offered by QuickBooks) allow you to back up and restore your QuickBooks data files over the Internet. This provides a great degree of security, but is the most costly backup option since you will have to pay a monthly service fee.

In the QuickBooks Backup dialog box, click Back up copy and then click Next

Select Local Backup and click Options to set the location

Click Browse to select the filename and location for your backup file.

In the Save copy or Back Up Company dialog box, click the appropriate drive in the Save in list (in these case we will use a removable disk)

Select the Save it now option and click Next

Verify or change the File name

Ensure that QBW Backup (.QBB) is selected in Save as type

Click Save to return to QuickBooks Backup

Select Verify data integrity in the QuickBooks Backup dialog box

QuickBooks selects Verify data integrity as the default choice for data backups. As the size of your QuickBooks data file grows, verifying data integrity will add significant time to the backup process. Consequently, you may want to verify data integrity once every few backups.

Additionally, if you are back-in up data over a network, verifying data integrity could substantially increase traffic over your network. Consult your QuickBooks help section if you have questions about this.

Click OK to begin the backup process.

After the backup completes, click OK to return to QuickBooks Home. If everything went well QuickBooks will show you a OK message

2. To schedule an automatic back up of your QuickBooks data:

On the File menu, click Save copy or Back up

In the Save copy or Back Up Company dialog box, click Save it now and schedule future backups and click Next

If you would like QuickBooks to back up your data when you close the program, click automatically back up when closing data file every..., and type the interval at which you'd like the backups to take place in Times or click New and set up a specific schedule

Click OK to return to QuickBooks Home

If you are setting up an automatic backup you should leave your copy of QuickBooks in single-user mode. QuickBooks will not backup data when in multi-user mode.

SoftCookies is an Intuit Developer specialized in QuickBooks integration software that brings passion, enthusiasm and high interest in quality in the software industry.

CHAPTER 9

How Do You Prepare Payroll Using QuickBooks?

How Do You Prepare Payroll?

One of the features of QuickBooks software is the payroll feature. You can prepare your payroll using the software. Many businesses are opting to have payroll in-house. The payroll process starts with the creation of your employee list. Who are your employees?

Do you have all the personal information you need? You should have the following information for your employees: SSN, Date of Birth, number of dependants, marital status, and address information.

How do you set up your payroll items? A payroll item includes the following: salary wages, hourly wages, commissions, bonuses, State withholding tax, Local withholding tax and any other tax.

You can set up payroll items at any time. The most convenient time however is when your company information is set up. This process may take time; so perhaps listing all your payroll items first may ensure you have them all.

What's Next? Next, create the accounts necessary to pay the taxes you withhold from your employees. You will need to set up accounts for federal, state and local governmental agencies. Your accountant can assist you with setting up those accounts.

Once the accounts are established, make a schedule for paying them. Most payment schedules depend on your total payroll and your payroll frequency. Many companies run into problems with payroll when the withheld amounts are not paid in a timely manner. Many times the penalties for paying late may be more than the payment itself.

QuickBooks software provides for various payroll options. Let your QuickBooks Solutions provider know what you need. If you need basic payroll help, online payroll, or assisted payroll. QuickBooks software provides the necessary options for you. Once you are setup properly the rest of the work is less time consuming.

CHAPTER 10

How To Use Quickbooks For Job Costing And Job Cost Reports

QuickBooks offers a plethora of standard job costing reports designed to give you the information you need to manage your customer and jobs. Some of these reports are only found in the Contractors and Accountants editions, but many are available in other versions of QuickBooks as well.

Jobs & Profitability Reports:

These reports can be found in Pro, Premier and Enterprise in Reports > Jobs, Time & Mileage.

Job Profitability Summary - This report summarizes how much profit your company has made from each customer.

Job Profitability Detail - This report drills down to the detailed costs and revenues for each job phase you billed to the selected customer or job, so you can see which parts of the job were profitable and which parts were not.

Item Profitability - This report summarizes how much profit you have made from each item or job phase you sell.

Profit & Loss by Job - This report shows how much profit you are making or losing on each job.

Unbilled Costs by Job - This report lists the costs you assigned to a specific customer or job but have not yet billed as reimbursable expenses.

Job Estimates Reports:

These reports can be found in Pro, Premier and Enterprise in Reports > Jobs, Time & Mileage.

Job Estimates vs. Actuals Summary - This report summarizes how accurately your company estimated job-related costs and revenues. The report summarizes estimated to actual costs and estimated to actual revenue for all customers.

Job Estimates vs. Actuals Detail - This report drills down to the detailed costs and revenues for the selected customer or job. It compares estimated to actual costs and estimated to actual revenue for each job phase you billed. That way, you can see which parts of the job you estimated accurately and which parts you did not.

Job Progress Invoices vs. Estimates - This report compares each estimate with progress invoices based on the estimate. For each customer or job, this report shows whether or not the estimate is active, the estimate total, the total invoiced from the estimate on progress invoices, and the percentage of the estimate already invoiced on progress invoices.

Item Estimates vs. Actuals - This report summarizes how accurately your company estimated costs and revenues for the items and job phases you sell. The report summarizes estimated to actual cost and estimated to actual revenue for all your items.

Estimates by Job - This report lists all active estimates assigned to a customer or job.

Open Purchase Orders by Job - This report shows the remaining purchase order line items that have not been received and their expected delivery date for each customer or job.

Job Costs & Bills Reports:

These reports can only be found in the Contractors and Accountants editions of QuickBooks. Some of them are also available in the Professional Services edition.

Costs to Complete by Job Summary - Once you enter how far along each of your jobs are, this report summarizes the cost to complete each of your jobs that have active estimates. It also shows how far you are over or under your estimate.

Costs to Complete by Job Detail - This report drills down to the detailed estimated cost by phase to complete the selected customer or job, and how far you are over or under your estimate.

Job Costs by Vendor and Job Summary - This report lists the job-related expenses you have incurred for each job, subtotaled by vendor.

Job Costs by Vendor and Detail - This report shows a detailed list of all the job-related expenses you have incurred for each vendor, subtotaled by job.

Job Costs Job and Vendor Summary - This report lists the job-related expenses you have incurred for each vendor, subtotaled by job.

Job Costs Job and Vendor Detail - This report shows a detailed list of all the job-related expenses you have incurred for each vendor, subtotaled by job.

Job Costs Detail - This report lists the expenses you have incurred for each job. This report is useful if you need to break out all material supplier purchases, all subcontractors bills, and all the labor costs for each job.

Unpaid Bills by Job - This report lists the bills you have not yet paid, sorted by customers and jobs. It lists only bills with an associated customer or job. This report is useful if you wait to pay vendor bills for a specific job when you receive a payment from the customer.

Unpaid Job Bills by Vendor - This report shows all bills you have not yet paid, sorted by vendor or subcontractor, and lists any customer or job associated with each item on the bill.

Expenses Not Assigned to Jobs - This report lists expenses that you have not assigned to a customer or job, totaled by vendor. Use this report to help identify costs that you may have forgotten to pass along to your customers.

Job Status - This report lists information for each active customer and job.

Customizing Reports:

One of the wonderful things about QuickBooks is how easy it is to customize reports and then memorize them for future use. At the top of each report is a Modify Report button. Here, you can change the way it looks as well as move, sort and subtotal the data in it.

An even more powerful feature is report filtering. Each filter represents a specific way you can restrict the scope of the report. When you select a filter, QuickBooks displays fields for you to fill in. The fields ask for information that QuickBooks needs to know to apply the filter to the report.

Once you have a particular report customized just the way you want, you can easily memorize it for future use by clicking the Memorize button

CHAPTER 11

Fixing Corrupted Data Files In Quickbooks

A QBB file is created by Intuit's QuickBooks software when the backup feature is utilized. These files are proprietary and cannot be read by any other software package available to the average consumer.

If you use QuickBooks to store and manipulate your company's financial data, it will become crucial that you take steps to protect this data. Given enough time, the most reliable PC will have some sort of hardware malfunction. But what to do when the company file becomes corrupted?

It is important to realize that using the same version of QuickBooks to restore the file as it was backed up is recommended and that trying to restore a backup file (QBB) using an older version of QuickBooks than the file was created in may not work. Obviously, you will need a computer with an installed version of QuickBooks.

You receive error messages when working in QuickBooks

QuickBooks shuts down when you click to save a transaction

Discrepancies appear on reports; that is, invoices or bills that post with a negative value

Deposited payments show up in the "Payments to Deposit" window

Balance sheet reports are not showing all accounts

Names are missing from lists

Transactions are missing

The company file won't open

Transactions can't be saved

You experience power surges or dropouts, abnormal shutdowns, computer crashes, or "Company file in use, please wait," messages

Not experiencing any of these problems yet? Press F2 to open the Product Information screen and check the number to the right of DB File Fragments - if it's higher than 10 it's just a matter of time.

It's extremely important not to ignore the signs because once a file is corrupted your company file may suddenly freeze up and won't open. In this case, you usually have no choice but to either restore a backup (you are backing up your QuickBooks file often, right?) or send the file to Intuit's data recovery team which offers no guarantee and often had a 2 week backlog.

You may want to start proactively working on keeping your QuickBooks data file healthy. One of the easiest ways is to frequently verify your data.

Verifying data

The "Verify Data utility" (Verify) is your primary tool for detecting data damage in your company file. Verify looks at each transaction in your company file and records a message in the "Qbwin.log" file for any damaged transactions.

Verify also detects damaged list items. While Verify detects many types of data damage, it does not detect all of the damage that might be in your file. You should run Verify in single user mode.

You can do this manually at "File > Utilities > Verify Data" but it's even better if you run it as part of a regular QuickBooks backup.

How to Verify your data

Close and reopen QuickBooks to create a new Qbwin.log file

Choose "Window > Close All", so that no company files or QuickBooks windows are open

Choose "File > Utilities > Verify Data"

If you see "QuickBooks detected no problems with your data", your data is clean. Click OK.

If you see "Your data has lost integrity", your data file is damaged. Run the Rebuild Data utility to repair the damage. You may need to run Rebuild two or more times to repair all of the damage. Rerun the Verify Data utility after each rebuild to verify that the errors have been corrected.

If your see "A data problem prevents QuickBooks from continuing", then your data file has a structural problem. Run the Rebuild Data utility to repair the damage.

Rebuild your data

If the company file is on a network drive, "copy" the file to a local computer before attempting to run this utility. Be prepared for this computer to be "unavailable" for several hours running the Rebuild utility. "Never" rebuild or update a company data file that is located on a remote drive (for example, by accessing it over your network).

To rebuild the file:

Choose Window > Close All

Choose File > Utilities > Rebuild Data

Click OK to the warning message requiring a backup of the company file before starting the rebuild

Do not replace your current backup. Intuit recommends using a newly formatted external media source for this backup (such as a CD or DVD). If necessary, back up to your local hard drive

If a message appears asking if you want to replace the backup file, click No

To avoid overwriting the current file, enter a new name in the Filename field

At the bottom of the QuickBooks Backup window, click OK

If the backup process fails, at the Rebuild prompt, click Cancel.

Do not continue the Rebuild process with your original company file if the back up process does not complete successfully. This can lead to permanent data loss

You must make a copy of the company file and attempt the Rebuild process again using the copy of the company file

Rename the copy of the company file with a unique name to avoid confusion with the original file

The Rebuild Data utility starts as soon as the backup process completes. Click OK to the Rebuild has completed message

Close the company file, and then reopen it to refresh the lists in the file

Choose File > Close Company

Open the company file

Choose File > Open or Restore Company. Then select Open a company file and click Next

Choose File > Open Company

Click the company file, and click Open

Run the Verify Data utility

QuickBooks makes it easy by automatically reminding you to back up your file after a certain number of company file closes. For instance, if you want to verify once a week and you open your file once per day, you can set QuickBooks to backup with complete verification (this is important) when you close your company file 5 times.

CHAPTER 12

How to Use QuickBooks For Job Costing - Setting Up Preferences and Items

Accurate job costing is one of the most critical tasks for managing job-based business like construction companies, professional services firms, and even nonprofits that are awarded grants. Many owners put it off because it seems too complicated or time-consuming. But if you're serious about helping your business grow and prosper, it'll help you:

- Analyze how each of your jobs us doing financially

- Identify problem jobs as early as possible

- Identify jobs that weren't as profitable as expected

- Create better estimates for future jobs

Luckily, QuickBooks is an inexpensive program that can do powerful job costing with the data you're already entering - as long as you set it up and use it correctly.

The first step to setting up QuickBooks for job costing is to set your preferences (Edit > Preferences > Company Preferences)

1. Go to Jobs & Estimates and check the box next to "Do you create estimates". You might also want to check the box next to "Do you do progress invoicing".

2. If you use QuickBooks for payroll, and every business doing job costing should, go to Payroll & Employees and check the box next to "Job costing, class and item tracking for paycheck expenses"

3. If you use QuickBooks for payroll, go to Time & Expenses and check the box next to "Do you track time". If you do time & material billing, you should also check "Create invoices from a list of time and expenses".

The second step is to setup your customer:jobs and use them on every transaction.

1. Go to the Customer Center and click on the New Customer & Job button.

2. If you are using Contractors edition, you might also want to create a customer called Overhead or

Administrative for non-job expenses, so you can use the "Expenses Not Assigned to Jobs" report (only found in the contractors edition) to make sure you didn't accidentally leave off a customer:job.

If you are using classes, you might want to consider doing the same thing so you can use the Profit & Loss Unclassified report to make sure you didn't accidentally leave off a class.

The third step is to setup items and use them on every transaction.

1. Go to Lists > Item List, click on the List button, and select New.

2. Add a new service item for every job phase you want to job cost. For subcontractors, this could be as simple as Labor and Materials. For general contractors, it could be quite lengthy: plans, site work, excavation, concrete, masonry, framing, etc.

In this case, you might want to add sub-items for Labor and Materials to your items if you want to track those costs separately. This also makes it easier to report only the Labor portion of a subcontractor's invoice on their 1099.

3. If you are a contractor with short-term jobs make sure to set up all your Service Items as two-sided, with both an expense and an income account. This doesn't occur automatically and unfortunately it isn't very intuitive.

You need to put a check next to "This service is used in assemblies or is performed by a subcontractor or partner" for the expense box to be added to the setup screen. Contractors often use a cost of goods sold account called something like "job related costs" for job-related expenses.

4. Builders and many professional service firms have projects that span several months or more generally use a work in progress (WIP) or construction in progress (CIP) asset account because job related costs aren't usually expensed until the project is completed. In this case, they should map the expense account to their WIP or CIP asset account.

5. Depending on your circumstances, there are also several Other Charge items you should set up. These don't need to be two-sided:

- If you use WIP or CIP accounts, you should setup two items: (1) Transfer out of WIP - with WIP as the account and note in the description that the amount should be positive, and (2) Transfer into COS - with COS as the account and note in the description that the amount should be negative

- If you accept customer deposits or retainers, you should setup an item mapped to a current liability account. For better tracking, you should consider setting up a separate current liability account just for deposits.

- If you have customer retention or retainage, you should setup an item mapped to an accounts receivable account and a negative for the Amount (for instance, -10% if your retainage is 10%). For better tracking, you should consider setting up a separate accounts receivable account just for retainage.

CHAPTER 13

Extending The Capabilities Of Quickbooks

There are ways you could expand QuickBooks' capability, how easily, and how reasonably. So, I spent time to learn the program in more depth and certified. Method addresses several different areas of shortcomings in QuickBooks yet you're paying for just one solution and can customize it to suit your unique business.

Here are just a few ways Method can work with QuickBooks:

You can have real-time sync - without having to manually click on sync, or File, Import, or anything other than save the entry.

You can access your QuickBooks remotely - and your QuickBooks data file doesn't have to be open.

You can have multiple users in QuickBooks but you don't need a QuickBooks license for each user; in fact you can have more than a few hundred users in QuickBooks Pro with Method.

You can have more Custom Fields using Method than you can in QuickBooks. And, you can use Custom Fields in Method where QuickBooks doesn't have any. An example is custom fields for Bills from Vendors.

You can rename fields. For instance, you can call Customers "Clients" or rename Classes to Departments.

You can customize data entry screens in ways you can't in QuickBooks.

You can control access so much better. In fact, you can even restrict their access to just a few specific transactions. And, this keeps users out of your actual QuickBooks data file

If you have a Mac user and a PC user, both access the same data file.

Method has a better audit trail; you can track who made changes to lists, such as Customers, Vendors, Items.

You can create drop-down lists, to either make data entry easier or to keep users out of other areas. E.g. you can provide a drop down list for a sales rep of only their customers instead of having access to the entire list.

There are three different levels of Method - remote, CRM and full-blown. Remote Access is the basic level. At this level, you can access QuickBooks, set up custom fields, customize the data entry screens, and limit access.

The next level up is Method CRM(Customer Relation Management) - you get all the basic features of remote but the additional features of a CRM package. Method CRM has two aspects: sales management and case management.

1. For sales management, Method lets you track marketing campaigns, opportunities and various sales activities. You can maintain your list of contacts right inside of Method but keep them out of QuickBooks until they become a customer or client - and you don't need to reenter any kind of contact information for QuickBooks.

Method CRM also integrates with Outlook including e-mails and scheduling appointments and events. From a manager's viewpoint, they can view a dashboard and analytics on prospects, customers and staff.

2. Some businesses need to track various technical or support issues with customers. With Method CRM, the billing can be created in Method (and sent to QuickBooks), but the specific issues, who was assigned to the case, status, priority, and comments are all maintained in Method. Again, the dashboard and analytics can help identify problem areas as well as successful resolutions.

In the full-blown level, in addition to Remote access and Method CRM, you get industry specific applications and a free form database. Two industry applications that come at this level are Method Warehouse and Method Field Services. As more are developed, you automatically get them - no extra fees.

Method Warehouse addresses some of the weak inventory areas in QuickBooks and includes the following features (this is the short list - there are more):

You can track multiple inventory locations.

You have automated bin creation and tracking.

You can have serial numbers

You can set alerts for critical levels of inventory.

Automated transfers can be set to LIFO (Last In First Out), FIFO (First In First Out) or FEFO (First Expires First Out).

Field service businesses may include pest control, HVAC, plumbing and electrical to name just a few. Method Field Services' features include:

Schedule one-time or recurring services.

Schedule by time of day or route order.

Work orders can span many days and cross over midnight.

Print, email and customize work orders and route list.

Turn work orders into QuickBooks invoices. Invoice one work order at a time or as a batch for a selected date range.

Group according to crew divisions or tech skill sets.

Track Customer equipment and serial numbers.

As a free-form database on the web, Method is already integrated with QuickBooks. For those who have done any programming, like in Microsoft Access, you will know and appreciate these features. You can:

Add an unlimited number of tables and fields.

Create and customize data entry forms based on custom or pre-built tables and fields.

Create actions that affect what happens in the software.

So let me give you some examples of how this might work for you. It was in seeing examples that really made me fully appreciate just all that Method can do with QuickBooks.

You could have a sales rep log into Method and see only their customers or the contacts in their territory.

You can have invoices put on hold until a supervisor reviews them before going into QuickBooks.

You can create pop-up messages for users - this could be instructions or notify the user that they did not fill in a required field, or a welcome message.

You could create a time entry screen that would have a calendar where they could choose to date a timer that they could start and stop as they work on a project.

When a user clicks a button, you can determine where they go next by the command underlying the button.

Sometimes, when customizing invoices, you need to have certain information for your customer and can't achieve that through the normal QuickBooks invoice screen. With Method you could have additional fields and additional calculations and put this information where you want on the invoice.

You can have your clients login to a screen you customized for them. They might be able to enter issues that they are having or view payment records with you.

I like to customize to suit my purposes, but must admit, that programming isn't for me. There's so much you can do with Method without programming. But, should you need the extra power, there are resources that can do the programming for you or perhaps you have staff that could do this.

Method also offers three different fee structures depending on if you want concurrent users, named users, or have users who need only a few minutes a day or month; this means you can tailor the fee to suit your needs. I haven't seen this with other software packages out there. Method also offers a free trial, so you can see how it could work in your situation.

CONCLUSION

If you're like most small business owners, you put on around 75 hats each and every day. And when it's finally quitting time, the very last thing you want to do is bookkeeping! I am with you - I am a CPA and I also detest doing my own books! But, I state a bold claim in the heading of this book - if you want your business to succeed, you have to learn Quickbooks.

Well, the bottomline is, in business, primarily small business, you have to know how you are doing financially at any given moment. Cash can be a scarce commodity sometimes in a small organization, and when you don't have a very good handle on the cash flow, you are basically sabotaging yourself and setting up for failure.

I have observed a lot more than my share of folks that start-up their company full of excitement. They have a vision in their eyes of how prosperous they are going to end up being and just how great life will be now that they are on their own.

They now manage their very own future and the sky's the limit. These people work 30 hours per day building their company - managing people, making vital advertising choices, ordering materials, etc. And it's very thrilling.

Nevertheless they put off maintaining their books, keeping all their receipts and bills in a drawer figuring they will do it on Saturday. Sunday arrives and they are exhausted, so they figure they are going to get caught up the next week.

The next week flies by in a blur and so they never quite get to the books. At some point down the line they find some time to do the books, however never actually learned how to utilize Quickbooks. And making it worse, now it is just so darn overwhelming they don't really want to even try it.

Next, after the honeymoon of owning a business slowly concludes they all of a sudden feel trapped in a job yet again - but now they are the manager and the staff!

Also to enhance the distress, even with all of the advice to learn Quickbooks and stay on top of the accounting, they never did, and now ponder the reason why they have $4.23 in their checking account and $5,800 in bills coming due plus a payroll approaching! Man, if I had a nickel for every single time this situation plays out....you know...I would be loaded!

You see, lots of this pain may have been averted simply by taking the step to learn Quickbooks and utilize some simple cash flow tactics. It's not difficult to do, you just have to take action and put it on the same level as advertising or sales. Yes, it is that vital!

So, if you are in this scenario, it's not too late...simply learn Quickbooks (it isn't tough to learn) and stay on top of those books. You will set yourself up for a greater probability of doing well!

www.ingramcontent.com/pod-product-compliance
Lightning Source LLC
Chambersburg PA
CBHW070402220526
45467CB00001B/461